Her side of it

Her side of it

poems by

Marilyn
Bushman-Carlton

Signature Books
Salt Lake City / 2010

for my family

The chapbook version of *Her Side of It* was a finalist in the 2005 Jessie Bryce Niles Chapbook Contest at the *Comstock Review*. Kathleen Bryce Niles judged. Previous books by Marilyn Bushman-Carlton: *on keeping things small*, Signature Books, 1995; *Cheat Grass*, Utah State Poetry Society, 1999 (winner of the Pearle M. Olsen Publication Award).

Acknowledgments appear on page 119, following the poems.

Design by Connie Disney.
Cover by Ron Stucki.

∞ *Her Side of It* was printed on acid-free paper and was composed, printed, and bound in the United States of America.

14   13   12   11   10   5   4   3   2   1

www.signaturebooks.com

Library of Congress Cataloging-in-Publication Data
    Bushman-Carlton, Marilyn.
      Her side of it / Marilyn Bushman-Carlton.
    p. cm.
    Poems.
    ISBN 978-1-56085-208-7 (alk. paper)
    I. Title.
    PS3552.U8228H47 2010
    811'.54—dc22
                              2010011737

We shall not cease from exploration

And the end of all our exploring

Will be to arrive where we started

And know the place for the first time.

—T. S. Eliot, "Little Gidding"

the poems

In the small town of Spring City,
Utah, during a plein air painting
competition my husband and
I watch an artist

at her easel. Her legs dangle from the tailgate
of her white Toyota.
We attend her like flies—
more than welcome here
as are sheep and horses, chickens,
and other rovers.
We see her smudge trees into being,
swipe fence slabs in,
brush sunlight on the side of a shed,
and listen while she thinks out loud
of adding something orange
between it and the shabby house.
It gets lovely as she goes,
as she gathers weeds
into yellowish bouquets,
scrapes a lazy line
to connect the structures,

and lets a single sheep wander in
to balance the turquoise tarp.
This makes her think the barrel
lying there on its side
should be red,
not the green Blaine and I can see.
The path she's putting at the bottom edge
is so anyone can ramble in.
We two grew up together
in a small town such as this
where flies swooned over buckets of milk
and hay was trussed into what seemed then
just mundane shapes.

—for Susan Gallacher

One

We retreated to

our private spaces.

—YANN MARTEL,
Life of Pi

Giving My Mother
The Feminine Mystique

"Not for nothing were they housewives."
—Ursula K. Le Guinn

Didn't she sing me out
the narrow door of her house
with all that pleasant crooning,

right through a narrow door of my own?

Didn't she lead me on:
blessing the yellow cupcake batter,
the looking-glass woodwork,
the small shoes, muddied to their mouths?

Didn't she conquer the cobwebs
with the squirming vacuum hose?

Where could I go but follow
the pointing stick above her hymns,

above "Springtime in the Rockies,"
above the "High Hopes" of the ant
trying to move the rubber tree plant?

And then I found something new.

I passed the paperback along to her
hoping to talk, two adults now,
sipping beverages at the kitchen table
with its bowl of waxed apples,

and just when her job was winding down.

Friedan's insights were old spoilers,
ones Mother had cored,
wrung out, tucked under, or cut up
and made into something practical.

And then, a daughter
laying it open on her mother's table,

pushing it through the lingering music,
diluting her perfumes of Pledge and Joy.

So She Wouldn't Fail

So she wouldn't fail at something big,
she kept busy doing average things,

things she wasn't ashamed to talk about,
exactly, things she could always say
were temporary, and just until she found
what it was she was really meant to do, or be.

Even the most desirable calling
had its drawbacks, and what if
once she'd made it there, she didn't like it
after all, and there was no escape.

She could see herself shut inside
an office, skin wrung out and gray,
feet itching inside three-inch heels.

Or traveling from one town to the next
selling something that at first felt fabulous
and then inconsequential.

She placed her belief in things
that could be inventoried: dishes, round-trip tickets,
brand-name blouses she'd find on sale.

Had she been a reader, she'd have liked fiction.

Her comforts required good taste,
but how exotic can exotic taste on a kitchen plate?

That was what she wanted—
to count on things that kept her busy
and beyond harm's way.

Most of her big dreams had been interrupted
or ended badly. Others simply passed her by.

But dreams kept pressing, and at their best
would feature her dexterous hands,
her brain with all its songs,
her kind compromising heart.

It was hard to live like this, she thought.
If only dreams had timers telling when
or could be scanned to expose the flaws—

some signal,
like a purple handkerchief in a breast pocket
or an emissary waving a white placard,
her name blocked boldly in.

—*after Stephen Dunn*

Women Made Up

"All women are female impersonators."
—Gloria Steinem

Make-ups line the counter like soldiers.
We're scrubbed to the skin and shine like fish.
The clock chimes remind us of time closing in.

Smells of Vanilla, Citrus, Cinnamon
project our minds to a Paris café.

Violet and Conch water faces and legs.
We wear rouges in shades of Monet.

This could be a Hollywood set,
real flowers shipped in, planted in dirt.
Polite ones don't ask.

Our lips are perpetually carnal with color:
Ruby, Raisin, various shades of Voluptuous.

The country fiddle and the violin
are the same instrument—
it's the tutoring that counts.

Pinkberry, Honeymilk, Dew:
women gaily arranged as mums at a death.

From innocents to end, our story's the same:
Janes and Marys come naked, glowing like chrome.
And then we must learn

lessons with paint
to disguise flaws that have come,

the arts of finger and brush
to flatten those impudent lines,

the abracadabra of Erase and Conceal,
to mortar the cracks fanning out
from Black Walnut eyes.

Just Men

In concert tonight, the four of them
are black and white

and Smetana's String Quartet No. 1 in E minor
overflows the intimate room
with grace and polished anguish.

Among the worshipping patrons
savoring this euphoric banquet,

replenished and lifted by their genius, I,

who am sitting close enough
that I could almost touch the cellist's cuff
or stroke his trembling bow,

become aware of human breaths:
deeply in, deeply out—

like those demanded by a doctor
when a patient's shirt lies crumpled on the chair—

breaths breaking out the phrasing
and swallowing up the music.

The Fallopian Tubes

My finger might be sliding down
the titles of the *Women's Complete Health Book,*
scanning the index of *Gynecological*
Pearls: a Practical Guide;

                         instead, I'm reading
today's *Patriot Times*
where I learn that the Fallopian Tubes
are a female singing group
who will perform this weekend
at the Blue Skies Festival.

                       My grandmothers
would blush in their coffins!
Even the word *woman* was brazen,
bringing to mind a plumb-haired jezebel.
They were *ladies* (almost whispered)
or perpetual *girls.*

And *their* mothers,
buttoned in from neck to stockinged arch,
would rush to cover their ears,
pump their fans, call for smelling salts.

I can see the group:
balanced and parallel,
like the ovaries and tubes
in their flat-as-Wish Bone-bottle hips:
spacious hips which mark them female,

pirouetting, and drawn attention to
by the fimbriae of taut cloth,
and by their very name.

The Fallopian Tubes deserve
a standing ovation—
the delighted way their tunes flow
along the muscles of their opened throats.

Yellow Smiley Faces
and Women

Do they smile in the houses
when nobody's there?

The Other Women

I'm the one tagging along
at my daughter's medical conference,

according to my badge her *Guest/Spouse,*
an identification that still stings with age.

When I got the chance,
I chose the traditionally feminine—

contemplating ordinary notions
in the shelter of home,
commuting to the kitchen and back.

Did I settle?
Use my children as a crutch
in case I failed?

Is my hyphenated name all that came
of a raised consciousness?
I walk against contemporary traffic

to meet Alisa after her session, through crowds
of gray males, the few gray peers,
and young females like her—

OB/GYN their badges brag—
who crowd me over
with their bright bags of drug samples,

and babble among themselves in tongues.
With syllables and sentences,

in temperate quiet rooms,
I write about my life.
If it were otherwise, I would not be who I am.

But I will never know what it is like
to be those other women.

Wife of Many Years

"She sees him, briefly, as a stranger might ..."
—Michael Cunningham, *The Hours*

You didn't anticipate
this occasion:

sitting in the audience,
he, set apart as in a clearing;
you, admiring his patient diagrams
and quaint jokes;

you, wanting everyone there
to understand who
claims his rib.

You've stopped hurrying for a change, behold
his pleasing architecture,
hidden rooms you often squander,

see him through tourist eyes.

No, you see him
in lambent afternoon light,

his outline colored in,
the half glasses on his nose
neutralized.

But why are you surprised?
Didn't his first valentine
tumbling from your crepe-papered box

make all the others seem small and dry
as cornflakes?

Aphrodisiac

You say you'd put your body
between mine and a smoking train,
carry me from a sheer cliff,
grab a wrench, or nothing,
and confront the noise in my basement.

But would you, My Sweet,
like Pierre de Châtelard,
write poems for your lady, be cinched
into clothes with collars big as carriage wheels?

Would you put on a tutu over snug short pants,
crowd your toes into pointy blue shoes,
flourish a garter below your left knee?

Would you enter my castle,
a plume in your velvet hat, pivot and bow,
spill your verse at my feet, if that's what it took?

Would you sweep me up,
charm me all night with a fine galliard?

Storm my chamber in secret, My Pulse,
patiently hide until I arrived?

If late, and in no mood to be wooed,
I called for my guards
and they shipped you to a dungeon up north,
would you still love me then?

Would your last words,
just moments before your head is cut clean,
be as gracious, as poetic,
as those of the Frenchman Pierre:

*Adieu, the most beautiful
and cruel princess in the world?*

Embroidering with Mary Queen of Scots

Some days I'd rather be in Scotland,
be locked in the prison castle with the queen;

in a circle with her ladies, ply a needle
in and out, and gossip

while the jail keeper rattles his keys,
keeps his nosey ear to the door,
strokes his forky beard.

The queen and her companions will be casual in serge
and buckram trimmed in lace.
I'll wear denim and an oatmeal tee.

We'll share legends, the story of Roland,
recite du Bellay and Ronsard, Kumin and Plath.

While her ladies weave their hair into bracelets,
Mary will work a bed hanging—
two women on the wheels of fortune,
one holding a lance, the other a cornucopia—
for Elizabeth, hoping to thaw her cousin's heart.

I'll work a pillow of a phoenix in flames
but with a secret message stitched in—
the date and hour of her impending rescue.

We'll wile the hours away
in balloons of sun through wavy windows
while Scotland grows greener, purpler,

the sheep get fatter, and Mary languishes inside,
never-minding the cannons cocked,
monsters in the moat,
hens beheaded in the kitchen below.

When it's time for the queen to nap, I'll bow,
pass the guard with the garlicky breath

and, once outside, brush a fly from my hair, the signal
for my spouse and chivalrous kin,

some hiding in heather,
some crouched behind stones,

some stooped in fields among nonchalant cows,
shaggy red wigs fringing their eyes.

Iguaçu Falls with Brazilian Nuns

Heaven bless the nine nuns,
their smiles popping from cinched

black habits. Bless their tidy
white lives, their jubilant faces

bobbing like holiday balls
on invisible strings.

Bless him who led the two of us
into their group—a duo

famous for efficiency,

known to havefunquick,
photographandpraise,
then pull our careless postures

on to the next splashing site.
Bless the nuns' first recess

in ten cloistered years,
the dark choking walls

of their contemplative order.
Bless their unsealed minds,

their lolling brown hems.
Praise each savored step.

When anyone comes
to something this clean,

when she snaps the atmosphere
with this much happiness,

she's caught me raw.

In the Kitchen on a Saturday Morning

Three men stand
in a circumference of slow dull sounds
of trade expertise,

repeat each other's names—
Tom, Mike, Blaine,
contractor, architect, husband.

Mingling with plates and spices
are the fragrances of just-washed bodies,
aftershave, detergents,
denim and soil;
nothing intimate or sticky.

If not invisible, I might intrude.

None of the three rushes to assent,
nor to fill in the acreage
between short phrases.

There are parts of the self to give out,
parts to keep in.

Weeks before tools will drop to the floor
and bits of wood inhabit the cracks,

before sweat broils in the brown wires
of their muscled arms,

they shift and divide the sum of their weight,
limber their knees,
unknot the coins in their pockets.

Occasional questions escape their mouths,
then flatten out at the ends of the lines.

Ducks on a Narrow Pond

Neckties knot
and wrap his look,

are tickets to the board room
where decisions are lobbed and nailed,

to the pulpit,
the White House,

to the starchy eatery
where napkins blossom from glass.

For the sly or wise,
the wannabes,
they are the essential slice of silk.

Loosened, they indicate men at work,
or liberated from it.

You see them roped around the mirror
of a car in mad abandon.

Like vanity plates,
they travel conspicuously,

tip us off
the moment he is introduced.
Some are megaphones—

yellow whirligigs,
flowers big as cookies,
fluorescent fish.

Some are shy.
Some merely drab.

Some simply state his habits—
bookworm, hockey, travel,

ducks on a narrow pond.

The Couple

You could almost envy
her uncomeliness
and inelegant flesh—
envy his exquisite
unapologetic tenderness.

Could love be less ambiguous?

If either of them were beautiful,
the beautiful
might be distractions.

They are too full
of gratitude
to be foolish,

too dull
to want more
than happiness.

Quarrel

      The newly-weds
enter the room like a trumpet,
its bell lip a magnet for the sun.

      Yesterday she drooped,
dragged heavy as a storm front,
came back home,
buried herself in the basement, cleaning hard,
hair wiping her shoulders like a whip.
We could hear boxes scrape the concrete floor
as she sorted and stacked,
sealed and labeled
mementos from her simple single past.

      But it's another day.
They come in tandem,
his misstep bagged, forgotten at the curb.

They dangle
and reach for the shine like vines,
their young leaves dripping with dew.

Two

I think I will do nothing for a long time
but listen.

—WALT WHITMAN

It Could Have Been an Impossible Day

And then the wind,
helping *Gardeners Eden* keep its promise:

the outdoor ornaments,
suspended from the wrists of the branches,
bump up and down,

emit "soft pure sound,"
the "pleasing alternative," they'd promised
over large wind chimes.

I'd sent for six in faith, not to be disappointed
with their durable enamel
cast-iron bird and pine-cone shapes

which arrived from Vermont
the first week of December.

After emancipating their metal tongues
from the stuffing in their throats

and levitating like a hummingbird,
out from the railing of the balcony,

I bedecked the withered wallflower elm
with their dangling silhouettes.

And there they'd hung,
you can't believe how still,
treading air,

half an instrument—
a violin in its velvet bed, bow in the shop,
a xylophone with shattered hammers,

a soprano short of breath.
And then the wind

wiping down
the curving ashy sky,

brings light blue Cs (the birds)
and a spray of pine-cone Ds
through the window glass,

each phrase like breaths in sleep
or the turning engines of sparrows,

like old departed ones,
their teeth clicking
as their spirits wobble up the front porch steps.

Let me be clear:
this is not aimless chatter,
an agoraphobic panic in response to silence.

It is not a lecture
on all they'd learned while hanging there
wide-eared.

Late March

Winter, sonorous and weighty,
chugs through the park creek over frozen
black stones. Snow bulges
the banks to bumpy old coats.
Bushes refuse to release their jumpy
young buds. You can almost hear
a prolonged restive sigh.
My daughter is cumbrous with child.
She can't remember how it was …

Ten Questions to the Tulip

Do you feel exposed
with your dress blown up
and over your head?

Does leaning sunward
show a bias?

Do you rehearse with the wind?

Do your lips ache
from smiling all day,

your toes from
clutching the soil?

Is there pain when a petal is plucked?

Do you compare yourself
to the lilac—her aroma,
her delicate fanfare of sparklers?

How many clouds can open their valves
before you drown?

Seeing the poem of yourself
in the rain's reflection—is that why
the top of your head comes off?

Do brief singing seasons
fulfill you?

Dust on the Limbs

1.

She's found a house. In my loose fist,
she widens her beak, drinks me in
with piceous-seed eyes.

Her feathers, color of dust,
break from brittle quills.

After a week in my care,
she can hop the clay sides of the saucer,
yet fears the wrong things:

shivering leaves, sun silvers, a split of orange,
not the dark jaws of the dog.

Though numbered,
sparrows have no apparent beauty;
their song is common as church grass.

Being ordinary is their province.

Some say *ordinary* is a word with no meaning,
but consider this:
her throat and squawk in a summer
so full nothing matters.

See a middle-aged woman,
a serious woman, on her knees seeking worms.

Hear her call a pebble of a bird
as it skips behind her over grass.

2.

The neighbors must think me daft,
wandering the black yard,

calling from the bottom of the birch
through stiff spruce and piñon,

into the dense shapes in the elms
that dance themselves free

from the thick July leaves of the London plane,
into every tree, for my little bird.

Four weeks from when we found her,
a featherless struggling thing,

she flies by day with other sparrows
that frequent the feeders in the yard,

eats with them from the soil,
learns their winged ways.

They should have warned me
that she'd imprint with my voice and with my fingers
dropping first food into her hungry throat,

warned me that, fat and full of feathers,
she'd stay this long in sight of the lit back door.

Usually by bedtime she's here on the step
or in the close loose arms of the flowering pear,

then sways to sleep on the silver swing,
her cage furnished with crumbs.

Into the empty night I call and call ...

    3.

She's caught
on a gray garden boulder

between the cries
of sparrows dusting the limbs

and me, adopted mother,
here on the ground,

maneuvering my fingers like magic crackers,
coaxing with the voice she's loved.

I watch her waver,
watch the quick switching of her head,

the black staring eyes.
I'm allowed moments here and there,

but she stays out most nights.
Her need to go—

how does she know she is one of them?—
is louder than our old tête-á-têtes.

I've been here before,
hands empty, bent over a nest.

4.

Outside in the morning, the sun not yet hot,
I'm eating my breakfast, feeding my soul.

There are beautiful birds
that come to the leaves in my yard,

brash blue, yellow, bonfire-breasted, and crested,
thumb-tiny hummingbirds hung in the air,
peppered quail in the feet of the trees.

She still comes,
most curious earth-painted one,

occasionally breaks from the dozens of others
for bread from my hand,
her claw marked by the dog's curious lesson.

When they float from the trees
to the flower boxes high on the house,
to the feeders, the sprinklers, the glassy green lawn,

their wings slippery and light,
I listen for the call of my own little sparrow
who knows who she is

and must pity her first love
here on the ground,

my voice puncturing her blue house of air.

Never Answer a November Knock

What is there to say of November
other than, between the popular colors of autumn

and the white anticipation of December
(ah, December, with spice and music

wrapped around her merry throat),
it can be relied upon

to show up in its usual boring slot
at the eleventh hour every year?

Gazing through its frame for thirty days
means gloom for even the breeziest optimist.

What is there to say of a time
when dead trees burn to chimney flakes

and leaves blacken in abandoned corners,
when green parks fade to pencilings?

I might enjoy it as a still life
but the artist is too fond of brown.

Girl on a Wing

of April.
to the top
all the way
of her parka
float on the buoyancy
you in. You could
chips of light that troll
She has such splendid eyes—
an I-just-won-the-prize celebration.
a look-he-loves-me smile,
a 90th-percentile smile,
Scribbled across her pumped-pink face:
her steps splashing the confetti-colored leaves.
piercing the cold,
her radiant blue parka and yellow hair
I pass a college student coasting against traffic,
at the bottom of this most demoralizing month,
Climbing Fourth South in November

Snow All Day

"If you want to make
  someone listen, whisper."
              —a commercial

Today I will eat only
mashed potatoes
and angel food cake.

I'll drape myself
in polar fur, linger

at the kitchen sink,
hands steeped in clouds.

I'll write a poem
for somebody blond,

wrap the mattress
in bridal white.

There'll be no noisy fire.

If you open your mouth
to proclaim it, happiness

can fade like snow
as it touches the tongue.

In the Loge

(a painting by Mary Cassatt)

It's all about seeing
and about being seen without knowing
and about who sees whom.

The woman in black is the closest
and first one we see.
Her face and dress

lack the color and lace
that would bring our eyes back
again and again.

Limply tied at her neck
is a matching black hat.
What catches our eyes

are the glasses held to her eyes
with one hand; the other,
clutching a closed gold fan,

lies in her lap. We see
through transparent gloves,
her ivory flesh.

Her glasses are trained,
not on the lit white stage
where baritones bow

and ample sopranos curl at their feet,
but on someone outside of the frame
whom we cannot see.

Farther back and unseen
by the woman in black
is the blur of a man in an opposite box.

He, also in black,
leans his white head toward us
and toward the woman. Like her,

his right hand holds glasses to his eyes;
his point precisely at her.
Both the woman in black

and the man in black watching her
rest their arms on the rim of the rail,
and are linked, unaware,

in the fuzzy impression
of a red heart-shaped
curve.

Them

"There is no wisdom without love."

—N. Sri Ram

We had come home educated,
thought that meant wisdom.
Hadn't we spoken to them,
shopped among them,
waited side-by-side while coin-ops
spun their segregated cycles?
Hadn't the myths we'd drunk
from our bottles been corrected?
When a cousin cornered us,
my husband and I stood together
as if to form a protective wall for them,
even though they were not here.

But she had just seen some,
a whole family of them. They were here
in a car, driving through town, down
Main Street, and back, then—slowly—
through the neighborhoods.
Behind the car, a U-Haul.
That cinched it: she knew
they were up to no good.
I don't remember what we argued
while our two young daughters
hugged our legs, only
that we raised blameless fists.

Much later
on the TRAX in downtown Salt Lake,
when we knew we knew better,
we turned away
from the two women with pendulum braids
and thick white stockings,
from the man with hatcheted hair and bleached skin;
from the thick books that hugged their hearts.
What part of which of us
mouthed some old fear:
Who are these people?
Why are they here?

Three

Think not you can direct

the course of love,

for love, if it finds you worthy,

directs your course.

—KAHLIL GIBRAN

The Quiet Ones

Guard the quiet ones,
the son whose pencil touches
the lines of his letters ever so lightly,

the daughter whose doleful songs
weave within the ordinary
language of her speech.

Their hearts do not burn before us,
nor shine hard and definite
like children's pointed stars,
but blur within a smoky broth of air.

Frugal, quick, their needs are hints,
whispers at the corner of an eye.

They speak without punctuation,
what they say falls away
like an interrupted symphony
or aborted bedtime tale.

Theirs is the faith of seeds,
seeds that sprout in the night
bothering our sleep.

My Son's First Day of Second Grade

Under auguries of alphabet and numbers,
his teacher laments her bad luck this year—
she has a ratio of three boys to one girl.
It will be a difficult year.

She has labels for everything—
Art Paper   Scratch Paper;
Coat hooks for *Boys* and *Girls;*
Paste   Pencils   Puzzles   Trash.

No place in her fussy design
of leaves on a wall—
the crimsons, oranges, egg yolks, creams—
for gray dirty leaves, ones kicked
or stomped to powder.

It will be a difficult year.

Three of the four in her classroom all day
baiting the girls,
yelling out answers without raising hands …

even the calm ones,
laboring out every last syllable
of every long word,

and squirming in their seats
like maggots …

Nickname

You feed them
as much good as you can:
potato water in the soup, pureed peas, beans,
ground chicken—sneak them in.

Their bodies ingest it,
marshal the nutrients,
which rise to fight colds, croup,
cancers, pneumonia.

You spoon mental bites:
Yea! You did it! Good boy,
compliment the skittish circles,
affix his pictures to the fridge.

He becomes a container
of kaleidoscopic bits:
prenatal vitamins, fluoride, calcium,
a reservoir of H_2O,

a multiplying body of self-reliance:
he can fix his own soup,
take cookies out and not be burned,
walk up to the clerk and speak;

can manage dogs, bullies, bad men,
back away from strangers' candy.

And so I was pleased to know
he'd found the sources of himself.
It was as if someone had scooped his body up
and shaken him well,

mixing all his colors—
his vitamins, his fortified skills—
and handed him some hot pads for shields.

He'd taken over,
maneuvered his first brush with authority,

had stood before the metallic teacher,
back starched,
and demanded:
Call me Jacob, please!

Joy of Spring

"Shouting for the joy of spring
and the shortness of life."
—Czeslaw Milosz

Here's my daughter:
ten-and-a-half and untroubled
under her cotton throw of primary colors.

Here she is—wizard of cartwheels,
queen of speed, and always a-tumble—
now holding her hands over her ears
begging, *Don't tell me!*
I'm too young to know!

What she doesn't want to know
are the facts
about a girl in town—

a girl not old enough,
and her boyfriend,
who are getting married.

She doesn't want to know why
this news
feels more like a meeting
on hard church chairs
than a celebration.

She doesn't want an explanation,
and I suspect she knows
how grown-up things

can be too fixed
for a mother's hands to mend.

She doesn't want to think about
her own bones bowing out,

or about the inevitable
stretching of her little-girl skin
that still fits fine, thank you.

Here's my daughter
bobbing sweetly in her summer spot.

She doesn't want to be pulled up yet,
nor to have the perfectly good
brown soil shaken from her toes
just because of an early storm.

Graduation

As morning breaks, our daughter,
wearing her best blue dress, is too excited to eat.
The wasted Cheerios bob like buoys in her bowl.

Though I've tried to tell her
that we have not been notified
or invited to the assembly—
that she is not one of the ten chosen
for the award—

she won't believe me.
She thinks I'm maximizing her surprise.

In past years when they'd paraded the winners,
then, when she'd resolved to make that honor hers—
that would have been the time to talk
about what's advertised
versus what's in stock.

We could have used a visual: a tower
of sifted flour piling high
on a measuring cup, then cut to size
with a blunt butter knife.

We, too, thought she'd win,
thought now she'll go boldly on to junior high.

We should have sat her down
and told her that nothing is certain,
that after the clapping evaporates

they won't remember your name.

Oldest Son

—for Christian

In hard natural light from his window,
my son dances. I've heard music

all morning draining
from his room, its ponderous
pulsing, the indecipherable phrases.

I freeze in the sliver of shine at his door,
holding clean clothes, and watch

the back of his freckled neck, watch
his elbows jerk and grind,
his hands whorl in erratic ovals. I watch

because I have never been a boy,
fourteen, shuffling into a man,

a boy supposing he's alone, a boy
throwing himself whole

into the unholy beat, music cranked
to complement his growing.

I have only been a mother
who has waited nights by this same window

while her son pushed back the hour
of his curfew, a mother

who has questioned the rhythms
of the great unknowable dark.

I watch because I have been a girl
in love with a boy this age,

because I have felt the thumping
of his heart and heard him
say he wasn't worthy of me.

The Girls' Game

The fathers think of soccer
as the usual battlefield.

They expect to see warriors
where little girls are.

From beside the sweet crushed grass
by the equator of the field—

where they see their own daughters
hesitate, lend a hand
to another who is down

and hear, *Oh, sorry! No, you go ahead,*
rise like doves from the din of the game—

they holler,
Get it! Get the ball! Stick with it!
The daughters hear them, of course,

but from inside themselves come
their mothers' cotton voices
and they can't make their own tongues stop.

Nobody speaks of disappointment
as the morning dew darkens the surfaces
of everyone's shoes,

as the fading fathers
hunker under sweatshirt hoods

and talk of the next game
as though they still have a chance.

Family Dynamics

He's left his journal open on the desk in his room.
    Passing by it
on my way to a closet where I keep frequently used things,
    I see it lying there.
It's personal, of course, and I wouldn't violate his trust,
    but a line,
a jolting one, jumps out like a red header in the center
    of otherwise banal lines
on post-adolescent living, that swaying bridge that is
    the path to manhood.
Those scared few words are begging to be heard, pleading
    to be lifted up
and rescued. I know it is his way of handing me
    the reins, knowing
I will go to him and have a talk. Then, because he
    knows the pattern,
while I am swallowing this unexpected information—
    there's more,
I might as well tell you everything, he'll offer, and then, according
    to the pattern,
he'll arrange to be somewhere else when I tell his father, whom
    he knows will react
vociferously and longer. Because I have had some time
    to mellow
and because I am his mother, and he, my baby, he knows
    I will buffer
the initial confrontation when his father comes to him.

I'm Searching the Sky for Cherubs

I'm searching for miraculous apple-faced children with wings.

Suddenly, after the long sob of winter

and a broken smile that wouldn't mend,

everything about my daughter shines.

Her skin is morning-moist, her laugh a bud.

I'm looking for cherubs within April's arms,

in her scattered dust of hyacinths,

in whirring wings that whisper notions

in her ear, for sleuths small as hummingbirds

cruising low to find the saddest hearts;

listening for convocations on a cumulus

where dimpled arms aim arrows dipped

in potions sweet and pink through caroling air.

love is a delicate chain of moments

—*for Justin in France*

Here, the heavy brown ones from your father's coat,
there, the ladybugs from Jari's first-grade dress;
and from your birthday shirt, five urgent reds.
You sorting buttons while I sew.

On a black magnetic board, I move words
into fragments, little poems:
travel the diamond road
recall together lusciously
incubate that vision
chocolate moon
worship delirious color

If I scan the words, rearrange and link them,
they become personal, as weirdly accurate
as a horoscope or class prediction, mythical
as kept buttons, true as portions of scrambled dreams.

Last night you were not in France
but in Brazil. The dream started with a samba—
a steam of green, sizzling yellow, orange.
Your father and I were there to bring you home.

here it rains like a bird
shadows crackle under light
magic has smeared a thousand pictures

The three of us were driving on a high road.
The moon was brown as a Hershey's Special Dark.
Not one clear star. We were holding to the path
of slick road and your father,
wearing that brown coat, kept the headlights off,
the wipers, too. True to form, I was fevered
by the height, my brake foot clawed the floor.

Though you are twenty-one, last night
you were small in the bucket of my lap, and accurate—
down to the heaped black hair and the red buttons
closing your shirt.

First Death

In her third year of medical school,
she's surrounded by death, this daughter
whose grandparents are still alive,
whose vocabulary hasn't needed words
like *malignant, terminal, interment.*

This week it's a man younger than she
with a clot that might move anytime.
She sees a heroin overdose,
a new mother with AIDS.

Now Al, one of her parakeets,
is suspected of cancer.
But just in case, she isolates him,
feeds him gruel, and he rallies.

Fatigued from having spent the night on call,
she finds him rigid, cold,
and phones in tears.

I listen while she tells of wrapping him,
soft and blue,
in clean cloth, of digging
with hands I've memorized
into the new syllables of soil.

The Smell of a Baby

Mom, she says,
this is my first one who has died.

I'd seen her cadaver
      that first semester of medical school—
      a sallow withered purse,
      one used long enough,
      then given to science,
      an old woman's choice.

      I remembered my daughter's attention to arm and leg,
      to muscles, nerves, tendons, blood vessels, ligaments,
      to the opened abdomen and chest
      and especially to the uncovered face:
      she'd honored it until the very end.

This time, at the delivery, the head and face are what showed first.

      In that luminous weatherless room of bodies,
      biting odors,
      the other students said they thought her cadaver
      had the faint smell of a baby,
      somehow the faint smell of a baby!

She tells me how she laid, in the mother's arms,
the cocoon of warm flannel,
still breathing then,
its face plump as a breast, as pink;
how she nearly forgot the confusion inside,
nearly forgot how its legs
were fused together like a mermaid's.
Later, the autopsy would show it was a daughter.

My daughter, awakened by a fresh life crowning—
one whose cycle would complete itself
in the time of a hospital TV drama—
tells of scrubbing her hands in the night,
of sheltering the mother, father, and baby
behind the heavy door
in a caliginous bottomless room.

Of saying,
Take all the time you need.
You can look if you want.

Contralto

—in memory of Nancy (Duffie) Furner, 1948-92

In the interval after the mastectomy,
before her head was a slick white egg,

she would color the gray roots
of her dark blanket-soft hair
with drugstore dye.

The scar wrapped around her torso like a hieroglyphic
and the damaged muscle
made it hard to reach above her head.

Heather, who inherited her mother's rich multi-hued
         mane, would help.
It became a monthly ritual: the two
shoehorned into the peach flashcube bathroom,

mother sitting on the toilet lid,
a towel hugging her shoulders,

daughter peeling the disposable gloves
from off the printed guide,

and then the girl gingerly applying the dye
while being soothed of worry:
get the roots, the black will wash away
from face and ears, from measled walls.

Though she still sang with the Tabernacle Choir,
she did not sing glop-headed at the sink,
but laughed her prosperous contralto laugh,
her abrupt rollicking resonant laugh,
each time the first shock of cold splashed her neck.

Black foam puddled in the sink.
From it, light mocked a rainbow.

Mother-in-Law

I didn't want to be disloyal.
It's why I didn't listen

when my mother-in-law
passed me her recipes for noodles
and winter squash pie,

why her house felt menacing
and dark, why I turned

up my nose at the foreign odor
of green cabbage bleaching on her stove.

She was not, and would never be,
the one who'd shown me how

to roll crust sheer as cloth,
to ease dough over a bent pie tin,

the one who'd sung to me as to a plant,
who'd made her hand a crib for mine
to teach the seven letters of my name.

I could not let this unrelated
surplus woman eclipse my own
mother's methods. I was alert as a cat

when I crossed the threshold of her house,
when I stepped over the invisible teeth
at the apex of her steps.

Sure, I'd pull her name behind me now,
but my mother's voice would reign:

Don't try to rush it,
or stretch the dough to make it fit.
Just let it settle over the tin,
as it will …

Having Grown Children

It's

                                                   lying   in

                             bed

                                   at

night

                    listen

                         ing

                   to

              the   wind   blow ,

          and

                wish

                        ing

         you'd

t   ied   the

                                  ai

lawn   ch   rs

down.

You, Me (and Bach)

Long roads threading through desert blush and sage,
skirting Las Vegas,
the calm before L.A. …

Enclosed in the car
with pour and pause of talk, we recall

a Salzburg concert,
shin splints in American Fork Canyon,
your broken Chrysler key,
love in a castle.

Tennis rackets rattle, mingle
with duffle-rolled T-shirts, shorts,
a six-pack of V-8.

Tires massage the road,
my fingers walk your neck,

unwind knots that lump
beneath your raven fringe of hair,
the gray insisting.

Your dinner jacket and starched shirt
hang over one door in the back,

my black sequined dress guards the other.

High-class scarecrows,
they keep the world at bay.

Old People

Our children are bringing them back—
those old people of our youth
who long ago diminished
to skeleton and skin, then altogether disappeared:

There are Emma and Elias;
Joseph with wiry brushes
where eyebrows should have been;

Isabel, my third-grade teacher
who shamed me all year;

Annie and Basil, Clive and Stella;
Herman who whistled when he talked;

Maggie, with her Halloween bowl
of wilted red apples;

Grace and Audrey, whose doilies
pinned to their chairs kept bits of gray hair;

Henry and Max in long loose pants,
their pockets sagging with white peppermints;

Hannah and Clara, Olivia and Maud,
wrapped in thin church shawls;

Sadie and Belle
balancing their lifetimes
on the dropped weight of their ankles,

shuffling forward
in today's fashionable shoes.

Prayer for a Grandchild

—for Holden at two

Let bells come
   from porches and throats
of brown cows

and whistles be
   handmade from weeds.
Let shock be

from stands of mint
   in a ditch and pansies
bearded with ice.

Let him find
   four-leaf clovers,
his name in a pond

of soup. Breathe leaves,
   eat snow, harvest
"cheesies," hear

ducks on the roof.
  Give him knowledge
of horses, calluses,

women in aprons,
  the smack of a ball
in a pasture, yarn,

copper dirt.
  Let him hear
music alone,

plain words.

Jell-O Boxes

Holden is just beginning
to learn his numbers
which, suddenly, are everywhere.

Of our visit next week,
he tells Amelia:
Grandma and Grandpa will be here
in 54 years.

When a son was in first grade,
Mrs. English had the class measure
objects in the room with Jell-O boxes.

Jacob learned that his desktop
was 6½ Jell-O boxes wide
and 5½ boxes high.

The chalkboard from one end to the other was 57½ lime boxes long.

He has lived 31 Aprils now;
Holden, 4 Junes.
He can count his cousins (7) and the
number of states (5 to 7, depending on the route) between Utah and
Maryland.

Are those frequent give-me-a-minute minutes,
60-second minutes,
or just-a-minute minutes?

And how many steps to the top of "hurry"?
How many years in a supper
when the soup has green things in it?

How many memories can I,
who have lived 61 winters—that's 3,172 Sundays,
measure in 2 phrases and 1 metaphor?

Noah on His Shoulders at Hogle Zoo

"... a vowel from the language of happiness."
—Lisel Mueller

Like balancing, way up there, a dictionary
with vowels and consonants escaping.

☆

Accidental and uncensored
like little hands on daddy's keyboard.

☆

Oh! the things we think he says.

☆

Sometimes cleaner sounds, but scrambled
like his puzzle blocks put like this:
the front of a cow / a pig's middle / a sheep's wooly end.

☆

Watching giraffes, Noah stretches his neck
and claps as his inventions
rub against themselves, mingle
as leaves turned on by a breeze.

☆

That same breeze rustling my own still branches:
his daddy on *his* daddy's shoulders;
from way up there, grabbing my own daddy's hair.

☆

Noah clap-claps as the silver seal slides easily
from the slippery wet lips of the gate,
then belly-flops into the pool, creating
splashes unabashed.

☆

There is no end to circles going out and out.

☆

Handsomely, he answers the rough-voiced lion.

☆

He fools with words like Webster did
and William Shakespeare

☆

or any enthusiastic traveler.

Adoption

—for Linnea

In a Marriott hotel lobby
in Guatemala City,
with green leaves growing
in the carpet
and a buzz of light overhead,
my daughter became a mother.

Her baby came,
sucking her tongue,
via the foster mother of six months,
who wore dark glasses
to hide her eyes

and who spoke,
through a Spanish translator
of the child: what
and when she ate,
when she napped,
what name they called her,
what made her laugh …

Then she handed her over
in a snug yellow dress
with one worn blanket
and a half baby bottle of milk

as if she were potted,
had tender green leaves,
and it was Sunday School
on Mother's Day.

PMS

My daughter-in-law says Elly has PMS.
That's because there seems to be no visible

explanation for why
she won't settle down for her nap

or for why she wobble-walks around the house
yelling "some sort of language,"

her cheeks pink as tiny good-cause ribbons,
her diaper bulky as a pamphlet.

Elly Elizabeth is one year old.
I think she has something to say,

but I don't want to argue with her mother.
Maybe PMS stands for pretty minor stuff

or purely manic squawking.
Maybe potty-managing situation

or petite misunderstood skirt.
Or maybe, considering the symptoms,

she might be coming down
with parroting mother syndrome.

Let Little Girls Sing

"How far that little candle throws
his beams! So shines a good deed
in a naughty world."
—Portia, *The Merchant of Venice*

Let little birds do what they do.
Let the rain of little girls' voices

flood alleys and cracks.
Let their elfish tunes—

their excited diminutive chatter,
like tiny bursts of confetti—flutter.

Let, oh let,
their two-and-a-half-year-old voices

purr. And isn't this the way
their stray pale hairs would sound
if hairs could sing?

Granddaughters chirp on the go—
circling snow
princesses, blossoms popping,

confectioners' teaspoons
spilling.

Once in Italy,
in a clearing in the Dolomites,
their grandfather and I came upon the tiniest chapel.
Amelia and Elly could be the choir,

dressed to soft bare feet
in white …

Four

Choice is restorative when

it reaches toward an instinctive

recognition of the earliest self.

—FRANCES MAYES

Do all of us have places

we believe made us ourselves?

—JACQUELINE OSHEROW

Love in Those Days

In those days no one anxiously
looked for love.
There was no ticking clock,
no talk of *settling*.
Because we were young

and not scientific,
we fell for black hair,
the brave one in class, the one
with arms dangling just so at the dance.

We had all the time in the world,
and the world had time for us,
giving us lazy years
to change our minds

without having to divide our stuff
or consider custody.

I learned things about you
you couldn't have told me
by listening to your report in history
on Dag Hammerskjöld,
seeing you lose an election.

In those days love was a verb,
a trickle of water,
an accumulation of inexpert stitches.

We didn't have issues
or hidden pasts. Love happened
in folded notes on lined paper,
in J. C. Penney school clothes,

while we carried books,
mine stacked on either hip,
yours clutched in a palm and swinging.

Naked

They'd come from practice at the gym,
their hair steaming, and in the flirt
and banter would reach inside
my girlfriend's car to ruffle our teased hair.

We'd swat their hands and laugh
(keeping one hand free to tug our skirts in place)
and slump our shoulders
when sweaters stretched too tight
across our breasts.

We'd scold when swear words came
from boys we'd known since grade school,
who heard the same modesty lessons in church.

It was spring, dirty streets, old leaves
oozing through the thaw.

The talk was cars,
and for an hour we traded Susie's Karmann Ghia
for their polished white sedan.

The glove compartment was locked
tight as their zippered jeans,
but the key fit,
and I began to read out loud
a pornographic story
from cleanly-typed and stapled pages.

It was funny at first, naughty,
an extension of our taunt and toy.

When I stopped reading, we weren't laughing—
those girls were not real,
just hyperbolized parts,
their faces incidental.

It didn't feel like love.

It was our initiation to the fleshy
underbelly of brotherly advice,
letterman's jackets, August kisses,

to the secrets that trapped their tongues,
kept their conversation small.

The Local Police Report

At sixteen, I'm listening
to sounds of a fractured frame house:

my older sister sobbing
over hard news
about a religious leader she has long admired,

and Mother saying absolutely nothing
so deliberately
the whole neighborhood can hear.

She's ripping worn towels into rags,
twisting from them dirtied water,

scouring previously perfect patterns
from the kitchen linoleum
and in such swift circles,
veins I didn't know she had
pop up and scowl.

To the tune of Eileen's sorrow,
she scrapes picked-over food
into the smelly trash,
fork tines squealing against plates,

then turns to bludgeon the risen white dough.

She chops carrots, potatoes, celery
with her sharpest steel knife,
and skins the onions. Oh, the many onions
she drops, tears splashing,
into the boiling pot.

Nothing We Needed to Know

And then, to show how it was done,
Mrs. Jackson, the home ec teacher,
bent down the way you drink from a tap
and demonstrated how to let one's breasts
drop into a brassiere. How each
should fall into its cup—
right and left—
for a perfect fit,
no adjustment needed.
She reached behind her back,
hinging her elbows,
and locked the fastener shut,
slid each arm into its loop of strap
and straightened: twin bulks
at the front of the room,
she with squat brown shoes, brown hose,
hair graying and tight,
the dress form headless and bare,
tomato aspic firming in the fridge.
An institution of baked eggs and etiquette,
a reputation as the toughest teacher in school
and the mother of two girls we knew,
in odd shapes of afternoon light,
a white brassiere on the outside
of her mildew-dark dress.
And no one dared laugh, not then,
nor later, when we sat, our chairs in a half-circle,
as she read, cover to cover,
voice pasty, lids low,
a church book on chastity
that filled the eighth-grade requirement,
but kept sex itself
an itchy gray blur.

Drill

In junior high
   when we were still
close enough to child-

hood to remember
   being unique, but
were no longer sure

it was a good thing,
   that WE were that
good—and we tried

to cover ourselves
   with identical
loose sweaters and all

wore ponytails and bangs,
   when our P.E.
teacher was just

trying to do her job
   and such conformity
made things easier,

when our class
    was to her like all
of the others, undressed

in the locker room—
    its flesh-colored bricks
sweating, its maze of lockers:

another fifty
    white mice—the fire bell
rang just as we

were about to step
    under the shower spigots
naked but for tiny

rough-nubbed towels,
    and we hurried to dress
before rushing the heavy

exit door to line
    up on the dewy football
field parallel

to wet boys in twisted
shirts and shorts, and after
the long bell signaled

us all back in,
Mrs. Walker scolded
us for being slow:

If this were not a drill,
you'd all be burned;
for heaven's sakes,

next time just throw
a towel over your heads!
Our uniform

shocked stares, then her
Nobody will know
the difference:

those mellifluous notes
and our unanimous
audible sighs

of relief ...

Straight Up

Shirley is the punch line for a joke
we comprise like pieces on a game board
in the line that wanders
from classrooms, through halls,
and around the walls of the gymnasium,
all the way to the dreaded shot station.

Holding dollar bills and marked slips—
diphtheria, polio, tetanus—
we rub arms we know will ache at recess
and watch the thin dishwater girl
with mottled skin
who always looks like she's been crying.
She does cry in the shot line, quietly at first.
When she spots the doctor—
his erect collar and white coat,
the way he holds the needle up
to check the level of pink serum—she sobs,
agitates our blood with screams,
and tries to bolt.

Remembering that she kicked the doctor once,
they hold her arms and legs,
force into her rigid arm
the medicine they say is good for her.

Standing in twos and threes,
we laugh. We know our times tables,
which way is north or south,
and read in groups, not alone with the teacher
in a back pocket of the classroom.

Every year she pantomimes our fright:
she does what we might do
if we dared
or had her reasons to.

After she is gone, the great room quiet,
we focus frozen eyes on those who held her down,
and take it in the arm,
straight up.

I Add Craig to My Prayers

It hadn't been a year
since he burned the tool shed down,
then crouched, crying, at the back of the garden
while firemen watered the flames.

And then they found the cancer
on his foot and took his leg just above the knee.

Just weeks ago I'd pushed him to the ground,
the devil alive and well in him.
He'd kept pursuing me like before,

then dropped his crutches
as they slowed him down.

He'd teetered like a sawed tree before he fell,
and worried me,
but then was up again and in my face.

The cancer has him now.
He lies passively
beneath a heap of quilts

his mother has moved to the front room.
His scalp is white paint.

Who'd have thought I'd go to God on his behalf?
It just seems right,

like the way his mother knows
to keep the curtains closed,

and how around his bed we use our reverent voices.

Cherry Trees

That good child, George Washington,
who grew up to be president,
hung huge at the front of the room.

It was February of second grade
and we were making cherry trees.

Stretched above the tidy blackboard,
all twenty-six letters
fit exactly round and straight
within solid and dotted lines.

Even the snowflakes falling outside
stacked in sequence on the fence.

Our desks were cleared and covered
with sheets of white paper
which we'd branched and pink-blossomed.

To set the paint,
Mrs. Putnam had shown us how
to dip them quickly
so the water wouldn't puddle
in the middle and spill.

There were girls and boys behind me
waiting …

Somehow water, lots of it,
slapped the floor and quickly rivered.
She didn't see who did it, but a boy
told my name. Jangling papers quieted.
A distant bell quivered.

Mrs. Putnam with round rim glasses
would sometimes raise her voice.
But now she shushed the boy

and led me softly to the back wall
where we hung my finished tree.

Later, she paused above my desk
where I practiced a row of small b's,
my flecked paper bruised and torn.

You're doing fine, she said, *you'd need
a ruler and compass to make them perfect.*

Guillotine

It was the Sanson family of Paris
who were trusted
through six generations
to perform torture and behead
thousands of unfortunate victims:
swords for the nobility,
axes for the commoners.

Then the guillotine, a quick and humane
form of execution, was discovered
by Dr. Joseph Guillotine of Santes,
who had once studied for the priesthood.

He took his information to Charles-Henri Sanson,
who had become something of a snob,
dressing stylishly in a green coat,
having petitioned King Louis XVI
for the title Executor of Criminal Judgments.

Between axings, Charles-Henri played
the violin and cello and was friends
with Tobias Schmidt, maker of harpsichords.
To him were given Dr. Guillotine's ideas.
"I hope this doesn't make killing too easy,"
Charles-Henri said.

☆ ☆ ☆

I am in grade school, far from France,
and the teacher has trusted me
to go alone to the supply room
with an armful of papers.
The room is dark and dwarfed
by the paper cutter, a large apparatus
with lines and numbers and a great blade
operated with a heavy handle.

I feel privileged, almost snobbish,
with the trust awarded me by Mr. Jones.
I sort the papers into thin piles
and set each one deliberately
onto the thick wooden square
close to the corresponding lines.

I pull down quickly
the great blade, thrilling to the graphic sounds
of slicing—almost an exhalation
or a last whisper,
a spasm of brisk grief as I execute
my brief commission.

Jesus Was There

In the frame on the wall behind the choir chairs,
Jesus was there,
as were the ladies
brushing the warm chapel air
with round cardboard fans.

And the men losing hair
and holding hymn books up
with rough sun-burned hands were there,

as were my father and counselors
and the stake president
in a special chair beside the pulpit.

And I, a white-stockinged child, was there
trying to keep my Sunday feet still,
especially during the prayers,
as they hung there mid-air.

The grown-ups kept their backs
straight to the benches,
the choir to its semi-circle
of pale cushioned chairs.

I knew why ladies' legs barely bent.
It was perfectly clear
for I'd watched my mother
dressing herself for the Sabbath.

From the girdle
under her best pressed dress,
rubbery garters dangled
and pinched into place
reinforced tops of nylon stockings
she'd carefully unrolled so neither would tear;

pulling one of the pair at a time,
from inside out with fingers and thumb,
beginning with toes,
moving over the knees
with habitual reverence.
I tried not to stare.

I knew about men
with the knots at their necks

and knew that for Jesus
even my father would wear thin manly bands
which circled, like elders at a blessing,
the white-root flesh of his calves.

He'd slide the fasteners—
copper tithing coins—snuggly along
with the tops of his argyles
into their slots,
which held them up, perfectly square,
like a sanctified prayer.

Garters those days
could keep any sort from slouching,
even in warm Sabbath air.

Always with Us

Years later at a high school reunion,
a girl gave a tribute to a classmate who had died.
Not knowing another way to end
her remarks, she did so
"in the name of Jesus Christ, amen."

I thought of Mr. Stone who was always with us:
in church on Sundays
and driving the school bus five days a week.

He sat at the wheel
in jacket and leather gloves, a blue, ironed shirt,
his hair leafed with gold.

On coldest mornings, he'd reward
just one child with the chance to sit beside him
near the heater. It was enough.

He kept his bus tidy—
no unclean or fractious thing was allowed
to enter his chapel on wheels
that, despite journeying children twice a day,
smelled always renewed.

Abruptly,
perhaps once or twice a year,
he'd pull over,
stop the bus, and with surprising passion
pull the emergency brake,
lift from the plastic pocket above his head
the tablet of rules,
turn toward the congregation—
even the innocent repentant now—
bend his head to necessity
and read them aloud,

always straight through from 1 to 10,
never raising his voice,
never commenting on any certain one,

never shaming who it was
who needed to be reminded ...

in the name of Jesus Christ, amen.

Carol with an e

Because there were wonderful things
she wanted, things she knew not to ask for
even at Christmas, Carol became
an expert swapper.

It was not without sorrow
that Mother made her return Linda Kaye Johnson's
transparent plastic purse brimming with
red and pink lipsticks, cranberry rouge.

When Carol returned with the old
family calendar, you could almost hear
the melancholy B rise from the piano
we didn't have.

Then she hid the black shoes with their heavy
silver taps and faded grosgrain ribbons
beneath milkweeds where the bus
made its stop. Mother never knew.

But they disappeared, and Linda Kaye kept
the blue parasol Carol had loved,
most of its bones being broken.

Finally my younger sister found something
she didn't have to barter for—an uncomplicated
lower-case e there for the taking
like one currant burning on a bush.

She began to add it to the row
of amateur singers in homemade cotton skirts
that was her name.
Mother let her keep it.

Though bent and stationed at the end,
that little e had satin in her voice.
She had a way of elevating the other girls,
bringing out a lovelier music.

Story Problem

From the deep well of his striped bib overalls,
Father would pull his pocket knife

and score the candy bars—
always two, always something

with nuts and stretchy caramel
and covered in thin skins of chocolate.

He'd divide each sweet bar
into six carefully equal pieces.

Much later, with five loves of my own,
I recall his careful measuring,

how he steadied the knife-holding hand
with the palm of his other

and bent to level his eyes
before making the final cuts.

He'd disregard what he knew
of the hour's bone-picked child,

disallowing any inclinations
to oversize the portion meant for her,

and would never undercut the portion
for the grumbling one.

For the fortunate child,
he was invariably more than fair.

Ladies' Food

Father has come in from the farm
more than usual this week
to rib Mother about her club-gossip
he calls it, or Relief Society.
He says there's not a drop of dust
anywhere in the house,
let alone behind the fridge,
and who will notice the bedroom curtains?
Do they bring their fine-tooth combs?
Some of their names—Wally,
Ora, Ilah, Roxie, Maxine—
pucker on his tongue.

Carole and I promise to make ourselves scarce
if we can answer the door
and lay the ladies' coats on the bed.
We'll listen from our room upstairs
for stock words, a name we recognize.
Mostly we'll hear them laugh
as we smell hot chocolate through the vent.

Mother is making *petits fours,*
and we help her press the five iced edges
into coconut and chopped pecans.
She assures Father there will be some left,
but he doesn't want this "ladies' food"
she'll serve on china from the top shelf.
He's already mocking
the new recipe she'll acquire,
and when it shows up for supper
he won't like it.

Nor will he notice the lingering perfumes
of chocolate and coconut
after the ladies have gone,

perfumes braiding for days through her songs

as she sprinkles down his shirts,
folds raisins into the batter,
and smiles to the window over the sink.

Learning to Be a Woman

We watch Mother empty pockets,
slide cookies into the oven,
wipe dust from the kitchen sill,
turn the cube steaks frying
(baby sister tucked under her ribs),
while singing a hymn from front to back.

She reigns in a cotton housedress,
smells of soup, shampoo, and bleach.

She knows where it is,
whose turn it is to be first,
how to spell *amnesia* and *cooperation*,
that carrots are good for eyes.

We see her spread butter to the edges,
set another plate at the table,
thaw chicken parts under the tap.

When an aunt or a neighbor stops by
and Mother must sit,
her hands reattach a black snap,
shape hamburger into a loaf,
measure paper for lining the shelves.

Sometimes we're shooed away.
Little pigs have big ears
they say, but they laugh, and the house swells
with the happiness of women—

they hug both arms, bob forward
and back, pink with glee.

Sometimes Mother wears lipstick,
rubs lotion over her legs,
dances her flesh into an elastic girdle.

Radish roses and little cube
cakes dot kidney-shaped plates.

The club ladies say, *Oh, Hon,*
your house is never a mess,
or, *Now, which one is this?*
Is the blond one the twin?

While our brothers grow up out of doors,
we sisters are framed by flickering curtains
or stiff winter ice on the glass.

We learn to sit still on a kitchen stool
while Mother dips a comb in a cup
and persuades our hair into curls.

Marilyn

Those milky moons I see above me
are the faces of my parents.

I'm in my crib, pondering my life
and the name they'll choose,
the name whose random letters are destined

to stand in line like second-graders
behind the biggest kid in class,
the appointed leader of the group.

They brainstorm from among the popular
girls' names: *Linda, Lana, Launa.* I like the L's,
the finale of feminine a's.

Rosemary sounds scented; *Susan,* musical.
Nancy, Katie, and *Cindy* seem friendly.
You'd invite them over.

But they're stuck on a name
I'd never choose,

and though they say it with affection,

I hear two brown splats,
smell wool, feel the tight wires
of eyeglasses over my ears.

With this name, I'm destined to marry once,
fly coach, get the chicken thigh.

Why not *Patricia* or *Kathleen*
which yield to nicknames?
Or something pious like *Ruth* or *Sarah?*

Anne with an *e* is my favorite, and I like *Jane*:
straight-to-it sounds of courage,
names always in style.

If I'm optimistic, though,
and squint,
I notice the coordination of the whole,

how the triple bearing posts of the *m*
look hardy and dependable,

how the tall letters stretch their bones,
how the round *a* balances.

And I do admire the *y,*
how she dangles her left leg
below the solid line.

Acknowledgments

The following poems first appeared in the publications indicated: "In the Loge," "Learning to Be a Woman," "Cherry Trees" ("Nobody Can"), "The Quiet Ones," and "Story Problem" in *BYU Studies*; "I'm Searching the Sky for Cherubs" in the *Chaparral Poetry Forum*; "Marilyn" ("My Name"), "Mother-in-Law" ("Daughter-in-Law"), and "Wife of Many Years" in the *Comstock Review*; "Learning to Be a Woman" and "Ladies' Food" in *Earth's Daughters*; "Dust on the Limbs" in *Ellipsis*; "Wife of Many Years" and "Prayer for a Grandchild" in *Poetry Panorama*; "The Girls' Game" in *Segullah*; "You, Me (and Bach)" in *Sunstone*; "Snow All Day" in the *Wasatch Journal*; "It Could Have Been an Impossible Day" ("Plain and Simple") and "Learning to Be a Woman" in *Legacy of Leaves*; "First Death" in *Encore* (prize poems of the National Federation of State Poetry Societies, 1997); and "Iguaçu Falls with Brazilian Nuns" and "The Fallopian Tubes" in *Utah Sings* VIII.

In addition, "love is a delicate chain of moments," "In the Kitchen on a Saturday Morning," "It Could Have Been an Impossible Day" ("Plain and Simple"), "Naked," "Nothing We Needed to Know," "Oldest Son" ("Christian Spinning"), "Contralto," "I Add Craig to My Prayers," "Straight Up," "Prayer for a Grandchild," "Graduation," "Jesus Was There," "Always with Us," and "The Local Police Report" all appeared in *Dialogue: A Journal of Mormon Thought*.